EXPRESSIONS

KEEP EXPRESSING, BECAUSE LIFE IS A BEAUTIFUL THING AND THERE IS SO MUCH TO EXPRESS ABOUT.

ANGELINA

Contents

Foreword	*vii*
Preface	*ix*
Acknowledgements	*xi*
Prologue	*xiii*
About The Book	*xv*
About The Poetess	*xvii*
Accolade	*xix*
1. Seemingly Forever	1
2. Mother	3
3. Drops Of Elixir	5
4. Black	8
5. A Surprise	9
6. The Impetuous Moment	11
7. Girl Child	13
8. Gratitude	14
9. Just For You	16
10. Untouched Me	18
11. Eternal Life	20
12. Bar	21
13. Streak Of Happiness	23
14. Unchained Mind	25
15. Not Me, But She	27
16. The Uninvited	29
17. Tribute For My Beloved Grandfather	31

Preface

When I began to write a Preface to Angelina's Book **'Expressions',** collection of Poems, almost the first thing that came to my mind were the following lines from Mahakavi Subrahmanya Bharati's well-known poem 'Vinayakar Nanmanimalai'

" O mind, perform these three for me:
Poetry is our profession and too, labouring for
The Nation's weal and not to rest for even a wink;
Let the Lord God of the Hosts, Ganapathi
Make our line prosperous."

Songs can be incredibly prophetic, like sub-conscious warnings or messages to myself, but I often don't know what I am trying to say till years later. Or a prediction comes true and I couldn't do anything to stop it, so it seems like a kind of magic.

As if the song is somehow speaking through me in its own language. And I am a conduit but totally oblivious to its wisdom.

That's why poetry, or even having the lyrics written down somewhere, is strange for me. The act of singing gives the most mundane words and phrases reverence and glory. You can make a shrine out of anything. The song has its own personality, and is bigger and stronger than I am. With more to say, to just write something down and let it stay there, on the page, seems to me an enormously vulnerable thing. And that's why poetry has in many ways turned out more exposing.

I don't know what makes a songa song and a poema poem; they have started to bleed into each other at this stage.

You can have everything.

-Mayoori Kango, Head of Industry- Agency Partnership, Google India Private Limited

Acknowledgements

Writing a book is harder than I thought and more rewarding than I could have ever imagined. None of this would have been possible without the grace of God.

Having an idea and turning it into a book is as hard as it sounds. The experience is both internally challenging and rewarding. I especially want to thank all the individuals that helped make this happen.

Although this period of my life was filled with many ups and downs, the time I invested in this book was completely worth it.

I would like to thank my family members **Late CHAKRADHAR SAMAL** for showering his blessings on me without which this piece of work seemed impossible; **Mr. Santosh Kumar Nayak**, my beloved father and role model, who always stood with me in my difficult times and always taught me to overcome all the hurdles that comes my way in order to reach to the final destination; my mother **Mrs. Nirupama Nayak**, for always being the person I could turn to during these years, she sustained me in ways that I never knew that I needed. I would like to thank my uncle **Dr. Narahari Agasti**, who always made sure that I am motivated enough to get the work done. He has left no stone unturned to encourage me and push me to achieve greater heights.

Specially I would like to thank my sister **Aradhana** for always being there for me in all good and bad times, her unconditional love gave me the encouragement and patience to complete this book with constant effort.

Moreover, I want to thank EVERYONE who ever said anything positive to me or taught me something. I heard it all, and it meant something.

Prologue

I am obnoxious to each carping tongue
Who says my hand a needle better fits.
A Poet's Pen all scorn I should thus wrong,
For such despite they cast on female wits.
If what I do prove well, it won't advance,
They'll say it's stol'n, or else it was by chance.

- ANGELINA

About The Book

The book "EXPRESSIONS" is a compilation of some of the masterpieces by Angelina, a budding poet of this generation.

These poems cover every aspect of life and travel.

There are poems on nature, environment, human nature, experiences and resonances. A specimen of her exquisite craftsmanship, each poem gives an insight into Angelina's life and the emotions she experienced.

These poems seem simple at first. However, as one reads, one begins to understand the hidden layers within. The words and meanings linger on.

Each poem will enhance the readers, imagination, coaxing them to interpret it as their own reasoning and depth of understanding.

About The Poetess

Angelina is a poet and author of short stories.

Here is her first book **"EXPRESSIONS"**, she has expressed some of the great verses of all time. Each poem is a specimen of her vibrant imagination, sensational lyric and thoughtful recognition and appreciation of beauty in everything.

Angelina, born in the year 2003, lives in Bhubaneswar- "The Temple City of India" with her family.

Belonging from a traditional family, she has inherited the deep philosophical knowledge from her father, **Mr Santosh Kumar Nayak**, her mother, **Mrs Nirupama Nayak**, and her uncle, **Dr Narahari Agasti**. Moreover, she has acquired the art of writing from her Late Grandfather **Shri. Chakradhar Samal,** who has penned down many books on different aspects of life.

Inspired by His Excellency **Dr A.P.J. Abdul Kalam**, the Former President of India and a World-Renowned Space Scientist, Angelina has studied extensively about the philosophy and mysteries of life and has made some important conclusions which have been summarized in this book under various headings.

As a POETESS her words create vivid visual images that add to the uniqueness of her poetry.

Accolade

"This dazzling book can take anyone's heart away. Exquisite book with so many interesting poems."

- Marshall Goldsmith, New York Times # 1 Bestselling Author, Triggers, Mojo, and What Got You Here Won't Get You There

"I am amazed by the quality of the content, Way to Go, Angelina, Wishing you a lot of success for your great work, 'Expressions'. The book is beautiful, the Type, the Cover, everything is classy. Great Product. Would recommend everyone to go for it."

- Amit Malik, CEO and Managing Director, Aviva Life Insurance Company India Limited

"Words are beautiful when you say them the right way. The book is spectacular and refreshing."

- C. Jayakumar, Vice- President and Head, Corporate HR, Larsen & Tourbo

"This is a beautiful book. I wasn't expecting this high-quality work from a new bee. A must buy for all poetry lovers."

- Prabir Jha, CEO, Prabir Jha People Advisory, ex- CHRO, Reliance Industries Limited, CIPLA, Tata Motors

"A classic book of poetry, beautifully bound and decently printed. A beautiful book for my collection and a must-buy book for all Poetry Lovers out there."

- S.V. Nathan, Partner and Chief Talent Officer, Deloitte India Job

"All I can say is, I am in love with this pretty book already! When I was given this book for review, I knew, I HAD TO BUY IT! This anthology is the prettiest among the ones I own. Her poems exude the natural freshness, the images it creates in mind are vivid and in maximum poems the tone is lyrical. Congratulations Angelina, for this amazing MASTERPIECE!"

- Ratan Bhardwaj, Chief Editor, Breaking News, NDTV

"Angelina is known to me for a long time now, I wish her Congratulations on her book 'Expressions', Angelina's work is well represented. There is a short, useful introduction that gives a brief mini-biography of Angelina and a quick mention of the sources that may have inspired her work. All in all, this book is an affordable introduction for students discovering the poet for the first time and an inexpensive way for older folk to renew their acquaintance with this extraordinary lady. I would give a 5 star for the content- that is the poems by Angelina."

- Dr Rajan Anandan, Managing Director, Sequoia Capital India, Head, Google India Private Limited

"It's a Beautiful Book. If you are a book lover it is really a collectable book. Outstanding, Awesome, Beautiful. I am totally Spell Bound."

- Amit Das, Director, Human Resources, Bennett, Coleman & Co. Ltd

"Ah! Bliss! Such a Beautiful Collection. It's for the old hearted who enjoys words to lighten the heart."

- Neharika Vohra, Professor, IIM Ahmedabad and Vice-Chancellor, DSEU

"This is a treasure for every seeker. Above all these poems are not literature but the rhythm of her heart andone cannot miss it. Whoever came up with the idea of publishing all the poems and to everyone involved in the process of making this. A huge thanks!"

- Dilip Chenoy, Secretary General, FICCI

"Great Expressions in a Poetic Style! This book is a Masterpiece. Dear Angelina, the content is above your age. I was spellbound by seeing your age and the quality of the content. This is just the beginning; you have a long way to go and a lot of success is waiting for you Ahead!

Blessed are your parents!"

- Prem Singh, President, Group HR, JK Group and Honorary President, National HRD Network (North Zone)

"It's a book which will take place, not in my bookshelf but my bedside and it's a treasure. Each page is new each time you read, deep wisdom in form of poetry which I fail to explain in words that are designed to open the eyes and the heart of the reader, and one that will enrich the reader's lives in subtle, but substantial ways. In this book, the reader will find out their empathetic gift, empaths, and society, the psychological understanding of being, nature, universe, nations and you name a topic which I guess has remained untouched and not expressed poetically with extreme wisdom! Every word, every page resounds with wisdom, depth, clarity, and pure consciousness. Astounding!

- Pradyumana Pandey, Chief Human Resources Officer, Mother Dairy

"The poems are simply priceless. I was able to grasp a lot from her words. The poems deliver profound messages in simple and few words. That's the best part of it. For it makes it time-saving, unlike all other

books where they simply dilute the message. Her poems are too deep, short and crisp and they keep on unfolding more and more as you read. Thank you, Angelina, for the amazing content."

- Carlos Medina, President, Google India Private Limited

"EXPRESSIONS is a book of poems that gives you joy, sorrow, calmness, wisdom, and deep thoughts.

Poems in the book are deep, intense, and thought-inducing.

Recommend? YES. If you like deep, thought-inducing poetry, this is the book for you."

- Sudhakar Balakrishnan, Group CEO, First Meridian

"Just holding this book is giving an extraordinary feeling of joy. It's like emotion to read such a treasure of poems by Angelina."

- Prof. Sayalee Gankar, Vice-Chancellor, D.Y. Patil University, Pune

"Wonderful collection of poetry. One must read this book. It will help to know what life is. Great piece of writing Angelina! Waiting for more such contents."

- Kavita Dasan, Chief People Officer, ABP Network

"This is a profound piece of work by Angelina. The book is very artistically designed. It feels great having getting the chance to write a review for such a Masterpiece of work done by Angelina. The wide variety of poems by Angelina is delightful. Feels like a collector's item, also the poems written by Angelina provides great insight and can be re-read."

- Aditya Mishra, CEO, CIEL HR Services

"You will start loving Poetry after this book.

This book opens the reader to the very essence of poetry, that every poem has multiple messages to convey.

Must read for a good lover of poems."

- Munish Kumar, Chief Executive Officer, Quess Healthcare

"Beautiful and Divine. The poems are so beautifully penned."

- Suresh Chandra Padhy, President and Vice-Chancellor, Poornima University

"Loved everything about the book, starting from such collection of profound poems from the various themes to cover so many aspects of life, it's an utter delight to read them, loved the overall aesthetics of the book. I would recommend it a must-buy for anyone who would love to explore the world from a poetic angle."

- Tojo Jose, Chief Human Resources Officer, Muthoot FinCorp Ltd.

"Poems with deep meaning. A must-have for all poetry lovers. The book is very sturdy and an absolute treasure for anyone who loves reading poems. Quit spending on gold, this book is the future gold!"

- Nivedita Nanda, Group Chief Human Resources Officer, Kaya Limited

"This book by Angelina is an absolute gem. A must-have for every seeker who is looking for a good poetry book. Every poem is a masterpiece. You can read any number of times yet never get tired. If you are looking for profound poetry, just buy it with no second thought in mind!"

- Anil Gaur, Group Chief People Officer, Uniparts Group

"EXPRESSIONS is the book with the collection of raw poetry and definite artwork which is alive and breathing, indeed a jewel in my

library."

- A.G. Rao, ex-Group Managing Director, Manpower Group India, ex- Executive President, TPT (Tata Teleservices)

"This book is not a normal book of poetry. It is written beautifully, Oh my Gosh! This is a great gift for anyone out there. I use it as a type of Oracle. I would recommend this as a must-read."

- Ashish Vidyarthi, National Award- Winning Actor, Founder, Avid Miners

"Beautiful Book, Amazing Quality, Totally Speechless. This is not a book of poems but more a book of spells. Will leave the readers speechless and wondering."

- Prof. Hiresh S. Luhar, Director, VIVA Institute of Management

"I love everything about this book. Even the cover feels good to touch. It is like a bible for me. Every night before going to sleep I open a random page for a good night poem. Simply must have!"

- Ashoke K. Maitra, Founder and CEO, Sri Ramkrishna International Institute of Management, Mumbai

"There is no word to describe the beauty of this book. Her poems are like a stream of consciousness. Deep and meaningful, also philosophical. You can tell that the person who has written these poems has experienced life in all forms and notices everything from minute things to greater things in the universe. There are so many beautiful illustrations that make the reading experience even better. I am reading a few poems every day and honestly these poems calm my mind and I cannot help but marvel at the words. This book is a gem and I think everyone should read this book"

- Harjeet Khanduja, Vice- President, HR, Reliance Jio

1. SEEMINGLY FOREVER

A piece of my heart
Walked away alone
Into the unseen, unknown
Scraping my soul apart
A piece of me
Left along with you
Forever into the blue
Until eternity meets me
I had plans for us
For months and years ahead
That I would have said
Had you been there with me
I had a notion of life
Filled with ups and downs
But now I say it with a frown
That because of you it became upside down
I loved you with my heart and soul
But now I hate you too
Because of your uninvited adieu
That shattered my life as a whole

I am as I was before
Now just without my soul
And along a heart with a hole
And with happiness atore
Once I did have faith in Him
Whom others call God
But now for me it's a meaningless word
That finds itself in hymns
I don't know where to begin
I don't know where to end
For to everything I tend
I dissolve into your thoughts within
Now at a loss of words
I put the pen down
And prepare to shutdown
Hoping to open up only to see you

2. MOTHER

Life was a dormant seed,
Until you watered me alive,
Time passed by with no leads,
Until l bloomed in your hive.
The swing and slides in your arms,
Got me sleeping,
While your lullaby casted charms,
Preventing me from weeping.
Those tiny steps l covered,
While u held my hand,
Preventing me from falling forward,
As you protected me with your wand.
The huge you gave me,
Will always be cherished mom,
Along the boring lectures,
That I heard when I lied.
The selfless love that you give,
With your enlightening kisses,
The kindness that I receive,
While you fulfil all my wishes,
Is something that I can never return.

So, THANK YOU MOM for all that you have done, While
I promise that I will learn,
To keep you smiling till the very last breath of my life......

3. DROPS OF ELIXIR

Millions of us rested together
Some big, some small
Some crystalled and some clear!
Far above from beneath
Far below from the sheath
Somewhere in between
Together did we breathe!!
Invigorated ....
We rose towards the infinity
Unseen, untouched
While caressing everybody!
Freed and spaced
We sought to win the race
Amongst those billions like me
Who dared to seek space ...?
Emotions were abandoned
As we fled from clasps atight
Apprehensions turned vacuous
As familiarity ceased ...
As distant distance dropped
And silent silence set in
Ambiguousity altered our arrays

Ripping the known apart!!
Soon the never-ending end ended
Thrusting huge responsibilities on our lifeless shoulders
Deporting us back to where we were ...
Our lives changed in a rush
We were all heading back
Unknown and unaware of our presumed destinations ...
With every flick of gravity
We shot down tearing the skies
With blazes and roars of our arrival!!
A blink here
And a blink there
With ruffles and tuffles everywhere
And finally, there we were ...
We pulled the sheets of darkness along
As we headed back to our beds
Casting our magical spells all along
Sometimes fast and the other times furious!!
With every move closer
I knew we were approaching new beginnings
With every passing second
I could see the next innings...
I thudded on a leaf
And slipped across it
Sliding and gliding all over
Covering vast spaces ....
With every account of mother nature

I gathered experience and beauty
Meeting thousands new like me
And then finally meeting my mother ... My sea!!

4. BLACK

You call it black
I call it absence of light
It seems to you dusty and dark
I see it when I lose my might
It's presumed as a hindrance in the vision
Though for some it encourages to see far beyond
In you it creates fear and apprehension
But to me it strengthens not to abscond
Protecting me as a shield from the eyes of the brightness / predators!
To some it represents aspersion
Though to me it is a savior from ill intentions
To you it might be a bad harbinger
But for me it is a universal acceptor
That picks in anything and everything given to it Without any complaints or expectations
To you this entire thing might be a hassle
However, for me it is an unbiased justification Thought to change our perception
And enlighten our intuition
So that each and every creation
Gets its true value and exculpation

5. A SURPRISE

As the sun dropped
Instantly the moon popped
But the lights went off
So, it became very tough
To see through the dark
As the dogs there beside there barked
I waited until my power drained
And then the wind howled until it rained
I was all scared
Alas! Everyone except me dared
To hold the darkness
With the hands of silence ...
Everyone but me enjoyed the moonlight
N I alone afraid ... Was sitting tight
Sweating like hell
As I heard someone ring the doorbell
I was asked to open the door
But I was the least interested to endeavour
Having found nothing, I retraced
When something up there blew up the mess
A letter old, antique and torn
Startled I went for inspection

As to whom was it written and why
Was it for us or some other guy?
But when I opened the letter
Reading writing, I could not utter
A surprise for my birthday!!

6. THE IMPETUOUS MOMENT

The synchronised chaotic strike
Of the arms of my clock and the sunlight
Made me jump out of my bed
Into the world of praise and plight
The misty cool dozed off-world
Looked really special and beautiful
With pin drop silence and no motion
As of everything was frozen and furled
All apprehensions suddenly vanished
As the cold gentle breeze soothingly filled my room To drive away from the bad memories that I never cherished
And gave me a new feeling altogether
Suddenly the clouds creaked
To reveal the ambiguity of mother nature Pouring tiny raindrops amidst the light streaks Turning the bright dry day into a wet street
With every drop of rain
I failed to understand the hidden magic behind That's soaked in it all my worldly pains
Without even caressing me This simple yet artistic scene

Pulled me into a magnetic world of poetic thoughts
Revealing a second aspect to all sheen
Without me even noticing its presence and essence
It was as if life got a second chance
With thoughts that my mind never pondered
As idealistic believes enlightened
Compelling me to retrace my vision
As realities faked out and deluded
And positivity engulfed me
It broke my day dream into bits and pieces
Waking a new me
Now the world felt earthly
As emotions redefined themselves
Harnessing me from the materialistic evils
Making me feel elated and scared

7. GIRL CHILD

Born to death
before it's very first breath
an innocent sacred soul
who has a by pivoting Role
It is not her fault to become a girl discrimination and crime
all against her without thinking
ahead which she tries to bear
times she tries to take his step
she is stopped with her mouth taped
why only with her
because of a gender
tell the answer
Or face the disaster
because she seems to be nothing
but from her arise each and every being

8. GRATITUDE

Billions had the chance
And millions did come to witness it
But I was amongst them all
Lucky to have found you as you!!
Patience was your posture,
Silence was your smile,
But when you did walk and talk,
Everyone feels dumb and did shut!
Every word that you spoke,
Did connect a string of our hearts,
Drawing me and my attention both,
To the world of your magic.
The striking glow in your eyes,
Pulled my attention in your classes,
Your refrains that of " KEEP DOING "
Did always imbibe in me the energy to go on!!!
Your flawless execution,
With perfection and garnished beauty,
And the taste of simplicity and aristocracy,
Did always fill my tummy, making my day!!
Thank you, sir,
For having thought of me as worthy,

And able to carry your knowledge,
Amongst so many who come to you!!
Your endless efforts
And seamless inspirations
Keeps me motivated all along
To reach my desired destinations!
I humbly bow by your feet seeking your blessings,
So that one day you are proud of me,
All by your heart and soul!!

9. JUST FOR YOU

You gave me birth
As well as it's worth
But took the pain all by yourself
Without anyone's help
You made me grow
Making me friends even with foes
But took the pain all by yourself
Without anyone's help
You gave me knowledge
Discovering it out of earth's every edge
But took the pain yourself
Without anyone's help
You built me as I am
Never gave my weaknesses a damn
And took the pain yourself
Without anyone's help
You spend more than half of your lives for me Without bothering whether I would fight or flee
And took the pain yourself
Without anyone's help
You wiped my tears when I wept
And you put me in my greatest debts

But I won't ever repay you back
So that I can have you as my parents for eternity as a stack
I am writing this poem
Because I have been said
Feelings are better expressed there
Where there is an absence of words everywhere
I owe my life to you
And hope you love me too
Forgive me for my mistakes
Which I promise to never retake
I love you mom and dad
So never leave me alone and make me sad!

10. UNTOUCHED ME

The darkness did ascend my throne
Overthrowing the reign of the fierce day light
That silently did revolt and bemoan
Trying to free itself from those clasps atight
The grip did loosen to wear my skin
Along with my heart that tore akin
Pouring my emotions out through my eyes
That kept looking for you through the shades of lies
The clock did chant hymns of distress
That made my beats echo out loud
For none of the sights seen did express
Any sign of silver linings to my dark clouds
My eyes did wander for you here and there
Looking for you each and everywhere
But you did seem more than astray
Coz, I couldn't find you even after hours of pray
The oozing time did pull away my patience with it
For my strained eyes couldn't find a single glimpse Of yours anywhere in the dark twilight
Making me feel now of dark spirits and jinxes
By then the moon did lose again and was forced to his hiding

While in the far end the sun did come riding
Slowly yet starkly, bright
Bringing in daylight with all his might
Just then a gush of realization did run through me Asking the foolish me to see
That it wasn't you who did leave me and go
Rather it was me who couldn't see you in the brightness low
And that you were, are and will always be with me From the very first till the last breath of mine
Never leaving me alone to flee
Even in sheer darkness although unseen!!

11. ETERNAL LIFE

Our eyes have never met,
But they were still wet,
When you were in pain
Our voices remain unheard
And the images of us blurred
Away across miles
But amidst this all
Across the barriers tall
We are and shall
Always be together
Our names may not connect
Our blood may not resonate
But we shall be one
And prove all myths wrong

12. BAR

The Sky looks blue and vast,
calling me to swim in it atlast,
but I can't move out
for my nest is caged
and keeps me highly bound
I am allowed to fly
to make sure I don't die
but not too far
within the bars
so what is they are bad
and they make me sad
but still, I have all that I never had
I am a free soul
who has to play many vital roles
as that a bond man and a Slave
but I am restricted and freedom is all I Crave
I am allowed to squeak
and let the secret leak
for neither can they understand me
nor can they feel
I do all I want
amidst there taunt

For they know what I want
and that I can't disobey there daunt
So what if there bad
and they make me sad
but I still have all that I never had the sky still continues looking vast
calling me to swim in it at last
but I can't move out
For my nest is dout and keeps me tightly bound
They feed me what they can
But just with a few drops of bane
there kind to let me use the things
but only at the cost of my Wings
so what if they are bad
and they make me sad
but I still have all that I never had

13. STREAK OF HAPPINESS

Hit by a heavy storm,
I was all alone,
Having lost all my form,
I remained from dusk till dawn.
No sight of hope did l find,
In the dark stormy night,
Nor a heart of kind,
In that unusual dark twilight.
Seconds followed minutes followed hours, days followed weeks followed months,
but no smile came across my life of dour,
Making My Life a mute Synth.
Soon my vision was blurred,
as I heard the footsteps unheard,
I felt as the world cluttered,
and my life once again turned absurd.
But then suddenly a shadow beamed,
as glorious and colourful as a rainbow, surely that was not a dream,
pumping adrenaline in my blood flow.

Words that were expressed,
stole away my heart,
taking the sadness that kept me suppressed,
separating pain and tears apart.
but that day remained just as usual,
when things began to change,
but I was hopeless and casual,
for that storm had made me the deranged.
Suddenly music field in the air,
and lights filled in the sky,
but I couldn't help but kept glare,
As I was surrounded by lies.
But somewhere within,
I don't know where and how,
That smile and peace crept in,
radiating happiness within me now.
It was therefore a feeling of Bond,
that will always be stored in the deep vaults of my heart,
secured by Spells of magical wands,
and a deep connection of thoughts and art.

14. UNCHAINED MIND

The nails grow long,
the eyes fierce,
with the hair wild along,
and the ears pierced.
a brighter Twilight,
without a motion,
in a dark night,
amidst black emotion.
silence around,
fading In the Rain,
with unheard noises as if in a sound, creating scenes in the brain that refused to be tamed.
the world grew black here and there,
in a silent lonely place,
while blood splashed everywhere,
increasing the heart's pace.
The bells chimed,
the footsteps Drew close,
the songs sung in rhymes,
getting the world to doze.

But someone's still awake,
with very tired eyes,
Forbidden to for someone's sake,
guarding truths from lies.
the clock chants tick tock tick tock,
casting a spell all around,
on with Beats as the chair rocks,
telling the time has come around.
but suddenly water splashes within,
Fading the figures things,
drawing the bleak light in,
confirming that I was dreaming.

15. NOT ME, BUT SHE

Drawn thin between the lines of night and morning
Fell those slowly emerging red rays
Just after the darkest hours, even darker than the evening
Feel those warn radiance on the sandy bays
The world around covered with deadly silence
Smelt lovely with the slow, soft, salty breeze
While the waves there clashed with rigid defiance
Trying to prove their strengths upon being teased
But not everything fitted its place
Not everyone there could see the nature depicting its poetry taste
For someone was probably running in an unseen race
Unknown and abandoned straining to find clarity amongst haste
She was brave or rather had no challenges to face
She was happy or rather had nothing to worry about
She looked normal probably because she had no grace
Or was simply emotionless without any doubt!!
As seconds jumped off her watch
She transfixed like a live scarecrow statue
That was fixed tall and straight amidst the unresting waves without a match

To help in the navigation of those work loaded canoe
The spry time changed never and kept passing by
Altering just the sky scenes from morning to night
But she remained there mundane and mortified
All-day all night without any change in sight!
But one day that seemingly bewitched situation
Changed on seconds, as if a lightning struck
Turning her face filled to bring with dissatisfaction
Add is demons ascended there bringing her bad luck
Not many things changed there
Fur only some strangers had appeared
Emits the light rays spreading everywhere
By the side of the girl who moved away fast, afeared
Days passed after that very day
And stars twinkling their above ransacked for presence
But never again was she spotted on any corner of the bay
Leaving the nature alone only with her essence

16. THE UNINVITED

Speck of dust around the end,
With millions as such at every bend,
On which I stand scared and afraid,
About words that they all said!
I am taught to grow up like me,
But they never allow the same to be,
Twisting and turning the threads,
Like of puppets, always dead!
Do I have a say?
No .... Not even in a single way,
Can I please be away?
No .... That's not how you are supposed to stay!
Numb and silent prayers sent,
Some said, some thoughtfully meant,
To those who don't probably exist,
But nothing beside them seems more legit!
Passion and fake profession,
Truth and false confession,
Are equally looked down upon,
Paralyzing once capacity to move on!
Not blood, not known,
Neither heard, never shown,

Stand always around me,
Not letting me be the real me!
However, that day is not far,
When I will rip apart all the bars,
And show all Kith and kin,
And the aliens too ... As to what lies under my thick skin!!

17. TRIBUTE FOR MY BELOVED GRANDFATHER

A person filled with radiance whose existence in itself is motivating and encouraging.
A person who taught selfless love and service and had always been out there to help others.
I am sure everyone who likes him is standing alongside with extreme pride and happiness to have been associated with him in some form or the other.
Destiny can't be changed and therefore we are sitting here with tears pouring down as we grieve together for my beloved grandfather.
We all know that he is no more with us to guide us or help us but we firmly swear to follow his lead in all walks of life and be the best we can be so that up there he will be proud and happy for each one of us.
His ideologies as a teacher, doctor, philosopher, politician etc. have always been cherished but now shall be our foundation for all the upcoming tasks that we shall ever perform in our lives.

Let us pledge to be honest, truthful, selfless, loving, patient, passionate and most importantly a gem like he was.
I am at loss of words to describe the big loss we have to encounter today but I request you to stand along with me so that together we will pray for the peaceful depart of his soul.
I hope that in our upcoming births we get to meet him the way he was always there as all: a friend, philosopher and guide.
His words and his actions shall be greatly missed. May his soul rest in peace. Om shanti!

18. MY SINCERE APOLOGIES

The dark silent Ambience,
turn over as the wind started roaring,
getting me to think about my transience, amidst the twinkling stars and the moon which was dazzling.
my memories went on a flashback,
making me smile for few seconds,
for the others untuned pieces of cack,
that remained in my brain absconded.
the clock tiptoed behind,
making a noise as of now,
probably because I had been blind,
and was in no favour to devow.
conversations soothed my ear,
While those images made me cry,
But I was in no mood to hear,
that these were my last experiences before I died.
The time meanwhile was taking dives, jumping from one of the hours to the Other, making me aware that it was high time to realise,
Else we would lose Each Other forever.

now the sun floated high up in the sky,
and I decided to set everything alright,
For we didn't meet to Wave Each Other a bye,
and that it was high time to end this fight.

Tips For A Happy And Content Life

Just keep these points in mind before you close this book:

- *Always know that happiness is always possible and you have ample reasons to be happy. Just sit up and count them.*
- *Look at your assets and your strengths, they will inspire you and make you happy. Be aware of your shortcomings only as much as you need to for improving and moving ahead.*
- *Be aware of the goodness of your family and friends, they can be your greatest source of happiness if you let them be.*
- *Never postpone being happy in the hope of finding yourself in a better or perfect situation someday. That day will never come. Life has its ups and downs and we can enjoy it with them.*
- *There is no end to wanting more and there will never be a stage when things cannot be improved further. Do not wait for that time or you will end up wasting your life running after what you do not have.*
- *Your peace of mind depends on your thoughts. Make sure they are happy thoughts.*
- *Do not let negative thoughts crowd your mind. Throw them out in whatever way you can.*
- *Condition your mind to think positive. Accept the world as it is and do not find faults with anyone or anything.*
- *Learn to be patient with yourself and others too.*
- *When you spread happiness some of it will come back to you.*

- *Never let small things bother you, it is not worth it.*
- *Always remember that problems are a part of life; they come and go. Do not get overwhelmed by them and lose focus of what is important to you.*
- *Do not get disturbed when everything does not go the way you want it to be. The world functions in its own way and it is wise to be a little flexible in your approach.*
- *Learn to be patient and understand people around you. Understand that people are not unnecessarily against you, they are not trying to harm or upset you. Even if they are doing anything that you do not like it may not be intentional. Try to understand them.*
- *Always remember, Life is Beautiful and you have only one life to live. Make it beautiful as much as you can, for yourself and others too.*

9 798886 410648

Printed by Libri Plureos GmbH in Hamburg, Germany